7·21·72

"WE PLANNED IT THAT WAY"

"WE PLANNED
IT
THAT WAY"

By Frank Knox

BOOKS FOR LIBRARIES PRESS
FREEPORT, NEW YORK

First Published 1938
Reprinted 1972

INTERNATIONAL STANDARD BOOK NUMBER:
0-8369-6726-7

LIBRARY OF CONGRESS CATALOG CARD NUMBER:
77-37889

PRINTED IN THE UNITED STATES OF AMERICA
BY
NEW WORLD BOOK MANUFACTURING CO., INC.
HALLANDALE, FLORIDA 33009

TO THOSE AMERICANS
WHO "FEAR GOD AND TAKE THEIR OWN PART"
WHOSE VISION AND INTELLIGENCE
HAVE BEEN AND WILL REMAIN
THE STRENGTH AND GENIUS OF THE
AMERICAN PEOPLE

Introduction

The writing of this small book has not been a
pleasant job.   It has not been a pleasant job because:

1. Any discussion of the New Deal concerns the mis-
use of public funds.   No one likes to think, let alone
say, we have in public office men who are guilty of
wrong-doing.   The facts are as they are.
2. No one likes to think, let alone say, we have in
Washington a Federal Administration that issues false,
and misleading, statements to undermine public confidence in private enterprise.   The facts are as they are.
3. No one likes to think, let alone say, we have in
Mr. Roosevelt a Chief Executive who has to be continually watched lest he slip over legislation depriving the
people of more of their rights.   The facts are as they are.

Often I have heard it said, just as you have heard
it said, that "Mr. Roosevelt is the victim of his own
advisers."

I frankly admit I once believed it.   I once believed it because I knew that in his job the man has
to have advisers; and he has to have advice.

But the mischief continues.

Up to a couple of years ago it was Rexford G.

Tugwell who was being called the chief "plotter." But, Tugwell has gone. Today it is Tommy Corcoran who is supposed to be the head man among the whispering brigade.

It is time the American people were realizing that all the so-called conspirators are subordinates — and, so long as they remain, will continue to be subordinates to the desires, the aims and the purposes of the one man.

It is time Mr. Roosevelt's supporters quit trying to shift the blame. It is blame that cannot be shifted.

The man who is responsible for the New Deal, with its objective of one-man government, is Mr. Roosevelt.

It is because I believe in our traditional American form of Democracy, because I believe in the capacity of the American people to govern themselves — it is because I believe these things — and it is because Mr. Roosevelt, by his acts, has demonstrated he does not believe them, that I have written this book.

The practice of democracy is a hard job. It requires vigilance on our part to see that those whom we select for public office do their duty. But, as a people, we've got to believe in democracy again if we are ever going to believe in ourselves.

If we are ever going to be a prosperous people again, we must be a free people.

Frank Knox

"WE PLANNED IT THAT WAY"

1

It was on a raw day in March 1933, that inspiring words came over the radio, "The only thing we have to fear is fear itself." In city and hamlet, countryside and country town, men and women listened, looked at each other, found strength and swung in behind what had all the appearances of being great leadership.

Party differences were forgotten. Republican and Democrat, alike, gave to Franklin D. Roosevelt their complete confidence. In return, Mr. Roosevelt gave them great leadership. A nation began to right itself.

Today, a little more than five years later, this nation is again in distress. Once more factories are idle. Once more 10,000,000 of our people are out of work. Once more there are bread lines. And this at a time when banks are loaded with money, and eager to lend.

What is the matter?

Why doesn't business go forward?

Why, if banks are eager to lend, doesn't business borrow (if it needs to borrow) and put people back to work?

Obviously, something is the matter. More than

five years ago we hired Mr. Roosevelt. We were told he was just the sort of guide we needed to get us out of the wilderness of depression. Not only were we told that, but the applicant himself showed us a road map on which directions were carefully marked. This road map impressed us. The applicant impressed us. So, as said, we hired him. We are still in the wilderness. However, we do have the road map, although our guide hasn't looked at it for a long time.

And right here can be found the cause for a lot of our troubles.

In the summer of 1933, instead of keeping the road map open before him, Mr. Roosevelt told us he didn't need it any longer — that he knew of a short-cut out of Depression Woods. It was a short-cut he called the NRA. In effect he said this:

"I haven't been through the short-cut myself, but I know it is a much quicker way home than if we follow the directions on this road map which some people call the Democratic Party platform. But because I haven't been through this short-cut myself, I want to tell you if it doesn't work, I'll try another. In fact, I'll keep trying short-cuts. I know there are a lot of map-makers who say there are no short-cuts. Don't you worry. There are a lot of short-cuts through this woods that these old fogey map-makers know nothing about."

Well, a lot of short-cuts have been tried.

We are still a long way from home.

And, while we are about it, let us take another look at that road map to see what our guide, when he was only an applicant for the job, told us about the direction marks on it:

Speaking in Pittsburgh on October 19, 1932, Mr. Roosevelt gave voice to the ringing sentence "taxes are paid in the sweat of every man who labors;" and, later, in discussing a plank in the Democratic Party platform that promised "maintenance of the national credit by a budget annually balanced," went on to say:

"I regard reduction in federal spending as one of the most important issues in this campaign. In my opinion it is the most direct and effective contribution that government can make to business. . .

"Our federal extravagance and improvidence bears a double evil; our whole people and our business cannot carry on its excessive burdens of taxation; second, our credit structure is impaired by the unorthodox federal financing made necessary by the unprecedented magnitude of these deficits."

That was true then. It is true today, with emphasis. But extravagance and improvidence in the Federal Government are not the only things that are standing in the way of a revival in business, with its consequent return to prosperity for the people of this country.

There are other things, not the least of them being the capriciousness of the guide himself. Not only does he try too many short-cuts across territory over which there are no short-cuts, but with the responsibility of the welfare of 130,000,000 people, he spends too much time playing with economic gimcracks.

He displays too much antipathy toward private ownership of business, and too much fondness for socialistic experiment. He says one thing too seldom, and does directly the opposite thing too often.

However, this is no attempt to measure a man. It is merely a confirmation of his measurement of himself, in words of his own choosing. These words are: "Remember well that attitude and method — the way we do things, not just the way we say things — is nearly always the measure of a man's sincerity." That measuring stick is found in a speech Mr. Roosevelt gave in Butte, Montana, on September 19, 1932.

Of course, you and I have heard it said, a good many times, that no President can break this nation, nor the business in it, no matter what his policies. That may still be true. It was true before 1933. But Mr. Roosevelt is ambitious, and he is equipped with powers far greater than have ever been given to any American President.

Awareness of how this power is being used is another obstacle in the way of business recovery.

Later, we shall discuss some of these things — "the antipathy of the President toward private ownership of business;" "his fondness for socialistic experiment;" "his capriciousness;" "his fascination for economic gimcracks" — in more detail, along with its effect upon the lives of all. For the time being, let us concern ourselves with:

1. How Mr. Roosevelt gained these extraordinary powers; and
2. What he has done with them.

To answer the first question it is necessary that we go back again — not to March 4, 1933, the day he was inaugurated, but to a date six days later, March 10, 1933.

On that day he made this request of Congress:

(*a*) Passage of laws giving him power to reorganize executive agencies;
(*b*) To lay down principles decreasing compensation to war veterans and their dependants;
(*c*) To vest in him powers to enable him to handle the entire problem of public expenditures in order that it might be done promptly and thoroughly.

"I ask," he said, "that this law go into effect at once without waiting for the beginning of the next fiscal year," and then he added this promise: "I give you assurance that if this is done, there is reasonable prospect that within a year the income of government will be sufficient to cover the expenditures of government."

Without delay, Mr. Roosevelt's request was granted. Some among the people's representatives in Washington looked upon this surrender of authority with misgivings — but, they gave it. Some among the people not in Washington were concerned over granting to any President — to any man! — "powers to enable him to handle the entire problem of public expenditures" but they, too, went along. "Perhaps," they conceded, "this man has some sixth sense and can pull us out of the depression. Give him what he wants so he can do it quickly."

The "reasonable prospects that within a year the income of government will be sufficient to cover the expenditures of government" was heartening. It was in line with the Democratic Party platform promise of economy in government. The Congress, and the people, still remembered how Mr. Roosevelt had gone up and down the country, fairly electrifying his listeners with his speeches and his promises.

Had someone told them that Mr. Roosevelt had just executed a political coup of first magnitude in anticipation of an entirely different program, no one would have believed.

But, by the capture of personal control of public expenditures the way was prepared for a program — as Postmaster James Farley disclosed in Detroit, more than a year later — that "was worked out in Mr. Roosevelt's mind before he was even nominated for the Presidency."

In case you have forgotten that disclosure, here is what Mr. Farley said in speaking before a Rotary Club luncheon and as reported in the *Detroit Free Press,* on June 23, 1934:

"Let me tell you there was nothing sporadic about this program. It was worked out in Mr. Roosevelt's mind before he was even nominated for the Presidency. He has known all the time just what he was driving at."

Considering Mr. Farley's position within the Administration, we must accept his statement as wholly true. We must accept it as expert testimony, showing that even when accepting the Democratic Party's nomination in 1932, Mr. Roosevelt had no intention of carrying out its pledges. Considering all that happened before Mr. Farley made this disclosure — and the very much more that has happened since — it throws considerable light into the corners of Mr. Roosevelt's mind, and his theories of government.

Remember that disclosure of Mr. Farley's as we go along:

".... nothing sporadic about this program . . . worked out in Mr. Roosevelt's mind before he was even nominated . . . known all the time just what he was driving at."

It will eliminate the shadows that confuse us. It will show the outlines of a man's ambitions standing sharply before us, with substance between.

However, and as pointed out, Mr. Roosevelt did not discard his road map until the summer of 1933. Then, in a surprise move, he swamped Congress with litter after litter of alphabetical agencies, and the propaganda accompanying them drowned out almost every business voice that tried to be heard. The NRA — or the National Industrial Recovery Act, as it was called — was the beginning of the real assault on business.

Overnight political coercion was grafted on to the American system.

Overnight Democracy was raped.

Just as suddenly as the coercional codes were imposed, the people began to hear that it was business, and business men, who were to blame for the depression that set in in 1929.

The machinery that was put into operation to discredit private business was the machinery of the Federal Government.

As a first step, that very effective political weapon, a legislative investigation, was chosen. In rapid succession laws were passed, practically all of them written to bring business men to their knees before the politicians. Paralleling these activities administration press agents laid down a barrage of misleading, or untruthful, propaganda.

By the score business men began their long parade into the committee rooms in Washington.

2

It ought to be apparent by now that the depression of 1929 had its roots deep in the World War. Likewise, it ought to be apparent that our present depression has its roots deep in the program Mr. Roosevelt perpetrated on the country beginning with the summer of 1933.

The depression which set in in 1929 was something we could not avoid.   In one form or another, war being what it is, and human nature being what *it* is, we had it coming to us.   Nevertheless, it was a depression that was widened, deepened and lengthened by our own greed.   For that we can blame only ourselves.

During the War we expanded to supply the needs of the world — and after the War we were not willing to allow trade to make an orderly return to peace-time needs.

Because we refused to face facts, and also because we had got into the habit of facing Europe, we still looked across the seas for prosperity.   For a time we got it, and we got it by a get-rich-quick method that was amazing in its simplicity and obvious in its unsoundness.

It consisted of lending a lot of money to people

who could not pay back what they borrowed. Of course these nations spent some of their borrowings with us. We were so delighted we loaned them more. Had we stopped to think we should have known they could not repay us. But who among us stopped to think?

Now there is a very human trait that almost always bobs up when something goes wrong. It is the human trait that compels people when they bump into each other to always blame the other fellow. That is what a lot of us were doing in the years between 1919 and 1929 — bumping into each other, not looking where we were going, not thinking about what we were doing.

We were crowded into one place, looking at pretty pictures. Curiously enough they were pictures made by figures jumping off ticker tape — figures that met our eager eyes and immediately translated themselves into all sorts of pretty visions of gold and silver, jewels, furs, caviar and long red automobiles. Then, just as the drama on the screen of our imaginations was about to reach its climax, someone smelled smoke and everybody yelled "Fire!"

Three years of depression fastened about us. Weary from hardship and uncertainty we began questioning. In Europe there had been kings and emperors to blame for the War, so dictators came to take their places. But lack of kings and emperors in this country was no handicap to the boys with the ready answers. Quickly they identified the existing Administration with hard times, and coaxed the people into turning over the affairs of government to them.

Cute observers of human nature, at no time did they even hint that what had happened had come because we, ourselves, had built a flimsy structure out of the lath and shingles of our own greed. Instead, they fixed the blame on the other fellow. For all immediate purposes "the other fellow" was Herbert Hoover.

In his campaign for election, Mr. Roosevelt was very solicitous of business — even to the point of crying that "reduction in government spending is the most direct and effective contribution government can make to business."

Looking around with his roving and appraising political eye in the summer of 1933, Mr. Roosevelt could see no political opposition that merited a second glance. But what he did see was that business was sure to object to some of his anticipated policies.

Herbert Hoover ceased to be "the other fellow." The business man took his place. The political attack on business began. It is an attack that has never ceased. It was well timed. As you will remember, in the summer of 1933 Mr. Roosevelt's word was something that seemed almost consecrated.

It is less so now but it is still beguiling, with the result that the present depression is being used just as the stock market boom was used yesterday. But, with this very important difference:

The stock market boom was used by private individuals in personal greed for money.

This present depression is being used by public officials in personal greed for power.

To repeat:

In 1929, it was unchecked greed for riches by private individuals that brought disaster.

Today it is greed for power by public officials that, unless checked, will bring a far greater disaster.

These things are blood brothers out of the parents of our own indulgence and our own indolence.

But, as to making a choice between them — and decent-thinking people oppose both — the former is preferable. When there is greed for riches by individuals it is the individuals themselves who pay the penalties for their own mistakes. When there is greed for power by public office-holders it is all the people who pay for the mistakes of the individual.

With all its faults the first system is immeasurably better than the second. Under it there is the certainty that the misdeeds of men conducting private business will become known, thus permitting regulation. Under the other system there is no way for misdeeds becoming known because information regarding them is choked off by the same men who do them.

And at this point it can be said there is no question but many large corporations had their pipe lines into Washington in the years before the depression, and during the depression that set in in 1929. For that matter, certain large corporations know their way around in Washington today. That, however, is beside the point.

The fact is, and the Republican Party can take no pride in it, that privileges were extended to large interests in all fields. That the Sherman and Clayton Acts were winked at. That big business got too much consideration, small business got too little consideration, and an unwholesome influence was wielded.

Mr. Roosevelt was eternally right in administering a few good swift kicks, well placed. The offenders richly deserved them. But that was no excuse for trying to kick them right out of their pants.

Mr. Roosevelt was eternally right in fighting to restore powers to the Congress. The trouble is, he did not restore those powers to Congress. He kept them for himself.

All of which brings us back to (1) the committee rooms in Washington; and (2) the New Deal propaganda machine.

Now, no one is maintaining that the people's representatives in government do not have the authority to investigate business. They do have that authority — and it is proper they should.

But, in common decency, no legislative committee should hide behind its cloak of immunity from court action, and make charges it knows are not true.

Using the old publicity trick that "names make news," the political investigators were assured of newspaper headlines by the prominence of some of

the business men they summoned; and, to make certain that the biggest possible headlines might be ob-
tained the accusations were so timed as to hit newspaper deadlines.   By inference, and sometimes not
by inference, business men were told:

"You are thieves."   "You are cheating the government."   "You should be put in jail."

None of these business men who were so flagrantly
accused of wrong-doing ever were sent to jail.   And
why not?   Simply because the charges made against
them were not true.

However, the real purpose of these Administration attacks was far deeper than a surface hope that
wrong-doing would be discovered.   Considering
the methods used, and the questions asked, the apparent purpose was:

1. To arouse suspicion against business men in the minds
   of people generally;
2. To destroy confidence in business management so
   far as stockholders were concerned; and
3. By search and seizure and demagogic appeal, to arouse
   labor against capital.

We were in a period when jobs were scarce.   It
was also a period when dividends were lean, if there
were dividends at all.

The advantages were all with the Administration.
Mr. Roosevelt himself took to the radio to discuss
business, and to refer to business men as "big and
little chiselers," "economic royalists," "selfish men"

— these being but a few of the terms that emanated from his speeches. Behind him there swung into action a political propaganda machine the like of which this nation has never seen.

This propaganda machine functioned under a Washington date line. You may not have thought of it but the advantage of a Washington date line bears a close relationship to the respect a vast majority of the American people have for government. Because they have this respect it follows that they believe what is said by those in the administration of this same government. There is real reason for this feeling.

For many years government reports were meticulously accurate. Administrations, both Democratic and Republican, took pride in this fact. Through the years the people came to know they could depend upon government figures and government statements. Through the years public confidence was built up until it became a habit for the people to believe official statements.

Now you and I know how hard it is to break a habit we, ourselves, have formed. It is correspondingly harder for millions of people to break a habit they have formed.

This Administration can be given credit for adroitness. It is fair to assume it was aware of this national habit of believing government statements. It may be unfair to assume it knowingly took advantage of it in giving out distorted and inaccurate information — but, unfair assumption, or not, the fact remains that many false, or misleading statements have been issued by government officials.

To be specific: The campaign against the public utilities. That is but one illustration of the sort of murder that was committed at the cross-roads.

Early it became apparent that the Tennessee Valley Authority was bent on destroying properties belonging to a private utility company operating in the area. To make the destruction more palpable to the American people — a large majority of whom still believed in property rights — stories carrying Washington date lines began to loom up on the front pages of our daily newspapers. Headlines along this line:

MUSCLE SHOALS POWER STOLEN

SCANDAL GREATER THAN TEAPOT DOME UNEARTHED

Over the radio, news commentators sped the sinister word that "preliminary inquiry indicates rottenness within private management of the public utilities."

One prominent utility executive immediately telegraphed Washington, requested a public hearing, saying, in effect: "If these charges are true, then I am the thief because mine is the responsibility for these properties." His request was denied. Nine months later a minor news item was released by the Administration. It stated briefly that "the charges had petered out, and had been found to be baseless."

The failure of the Administration to make good

on its charges seemingly was of no moment. The damage was done. The newspaper headline attack had accomplished its purpose. Under cover of its lurid charges it was able to appropriate millions upon millions of dollars to the Tennessee Valley Authority, and to embark on an experiment that Norman Thomas, perennial Socialist candiate for the Presidency, has called "pure Socialism." By its lurid charges it undermined public confidence in the public utility business and drove down the market value of stocks, thus causing further losses to the stockholders. By so doing it made it much easier to put government into business in competition with its own citizens, and to the inevitable destruction of private ownership of the utilities.

Miss Dorothy Thompson, in one of her syndicated newspaper columns, summed it up this way:

"Unfortunately our policies are made by people who are often sadistic anti-capitalists. . . They seem to think that the way to socialize any industry is first to bankrupt it and then socialize the losses."

"Sadistic anti-capitalistism" is illustrative of the methods used in the working out of the program Mr. Roosevelt "had in mind long before he was even nominated." It is also illustrative of the effectiveness of the New Deal's propaganda machine, once it swings into action. As already said, this is a political propaganda machine the like of which this country has never before seen.

This, too, is something that has been built since

March 10, 1933, when Congress gave to Mr. Roosevelt "powers to handle the entire problem of public expenditures."

In June 1937, the non-political and fact-finding Brookings Institute reported on this New Deal propaganda machine as follows:

"No figures are available on the growth of publicity activities, but it is evident that it has increased materially in recent years. . . Reports received from the executive agencies show that during the fiscal year 1936 the expenditures for salaries of persons who were engaged solely in publicity work or a part of whose time was allocated to that purpose amounted to $521,000. In addition the salaries of persons who were employed partly on publicity work, but whose time was not allocated, amounted to $81,000. These figures are for salaries of office staff only and do not include any expenditures for salaries, equipment and supplies used in duplicating the releases. . .

"The figures above do not include any for the Works Progress Administration, which has not submitted a report on these activities. The figures likewise do not cover offices outside the District of Columbia, with the exception of the Tennessee Valley Authority."

When a fact-finding and non-political body such as the Brookings Institute is compelled to report that "no figures are available," you may be sure that all the facts, and figures, of the New Deal propaganda organization are going to be difficult for any citizen to locate.

But enough is known to make it certain that the $602,000 spent in 1936 for "office staff only in

Washington" is an exceedingly small part of the total cost of telling the people that:

1. Mr. Roosevelt is a great President; and
2. The New Deal is a great idealistic program.

There are Administration propaganda agencies in every one of the 48 states. The purpose of these sub-agencies (for Washington is the clearing house for all) is to spread the gospel of the New Movement and its Leader. These sub-agencies also act as sentries for the Commander-in-chief, reporting any hostile or suspicious movement in the camp of the citizenry.

Let a person of prominence speak up in criticism of the New Deal and any one of three things — or, all three — is likely to happen to him:

1. In due time he will find himself before a legislative committee in Washington;
2. he will be publicly castigated by an obedient office-holder in Washington; and/or
3. he will be put on the calling list of the Internal Revenue Department.

Punishments Number 1 and 2, in the technique of the New Deal propaganda methods, are known as "getting a Washington date line." Its effectiveness has been pointed out. Punishment Number 3 is no less effective. Even in failure the Administration has a hard time losing. If nothing can be found wrong with the citizen's tax return the usual effect is that he is so completely awed by the belligerency of the Internal Revenue Department's investigators that he decides thereafter to keep still. On the other hand, if some error is discovered, there are house-tops, and a Capitol Dome, from which to shout it — and, again, the Washington date line technique.

These sub-agencies of the New Deal's propaganda machine also serve other purposes. One is to keep in close contact with all the newspaper editors, and reporters, in their district, supplying them with all sorts of press handouts to write letters to the editor protesting any criticism of the New Deal to supply background material to Washington on any and all spending that is contemplated in a selected area; and to supply New Deal Senators and Congressmen — again for use under a Washington date line — with direct quotations from identified local politicians praising this or that federal project.

These are but a few of the duties of the Press Agentry of the New Movement. To enumerate these duties would require a book much larger than this one. To even identify the propaganda agencies would fill many pages; but an inkling of the number can be given by merely stating there are close to seventy whose identification comes under the heading of only the first three letters in the alphabet.

Every conceivable form of propaganda is used: books and booklets, billboards, magazines and newspapers, motion pictures and radio programs, personal contact by thousands of field representatives, circulating constantly by airplane, by train, by automobile, on horseback and on foot. To attempt to estimate the cost of all this effort would be to indulge in guesswork.

But, a number of statements can be made that are not based on guesswork:

1. Glorifying propaganda of this nature is also the technique of the Communists, the Nazists and the Fascists;
2. The New Deal propaganda machine is the equal, if not the superior, of the machines set up to praise Stalin, Hitler and Mussolini;
3. It is a machine that functions along lines quite similar to the organizations of Stalin, Hitler and Mussolini;
4. It is a machine which has been set up in open contempt of laws prohibiting using public funds this way.

Because it is a serious charge to accuse public officials of misusing public funds, I wish to elaborate this fourth statement.

And, in elaborating, may I thank Mr. Roy W. Howard, Editor of the independent Scripps-Howard newspapers, for the publication of a series of articles, showing that from $25,000,000 to $40,-000,000 of the people's money is being spent each year to exploit the Administration.

The law which was referred to in the articles published in Mr. Howard's newspapers was passed on October 22, 1913. Under it, "no money appropriated by any Act shall be used for compensation of any publicity expert unless specifically appropriated for that purpose."

There have been no such specific appropriations.

In fact, on March 8, 1938, Representative Thomas, of New Jersey, introduced a resolution empowering the Speaker of the House of Representatives to investigate the question of publicity, and the dissemination of propaganda by Executive Agencies for the purpose of determining to what extent, if any, "the existing Statute has been violated."

No favorable action was taken.

On June 3, 1938, Senator Austin, of Vermont, introduced an amendment to a pending Joint Resolution, section (a), which read:

"No part of any appropriation in this Act shall be used for any political purpose, and no authority conferred by this Act upon any person shall be exercised or administered for any such purpose."

The amendment was rejected.

On March 23, 1934, Representative Fish, of New York, introduced a Resolution providing for an inquiry into the publicity activities of the New Deal.

No action was taken on this Resolution.

At approximately the same time, or in the spring of 1934, Senator King, of Utah, introduced a Resolution calling for much the same information.

No action was taken on this Resolution.

Nor, have these been the only attempts made by the people's representatives in the Congress to force the Administration to obey the law. All such attempts have met with failure.

Personally, I am of the belief that the President of the United States should be the *first* among us to obey the law.

5. Also, in addition to being a propaganda organization, it is an espionage system in full bloom, in a nation that is still a Democracy.

This propaganda machine is set up so it can attack immediately on the forty-eight fronts in the forty-eight states, as well as in Alaska, Puerto Rico, Hawaii and the Virgin Islands. In the din raised by its shouting voices, it is difficult for those who still believe in private ownership of property to make themselves heard. It is exceedingly difficult for those who want to work at a profit to themselves, and to their employes, to stay in business.

The laws have been so fixed, that when the propaganda machine and the legislative investigating committees fail, the tax collector succeeds.

3

Since March 4, 1933, Franklin D. Roosevelt has spent, in round figures, $40,000,000,000. By the time his second term ends, it is almost certain he will have spent an additional $25,000,000,000. Together, that makes a total of $65,000,000,000!

Of $40,000,000,000 already spent, $24,500,000,-000 was collected. The remaining $15,500,000,000 is debt.

Of the $25,000,000,000 Mr. Roosevelt is almost certain to spend by the time he completes his second term in office, $15,000,000,000 is the approximate sum that will be collected. The additional $10,000-000,000 will be debt.

This means that by the time Mr. Roosevelt completes his second term, the national debt will have increased from $20,934,728,350 in March 1933, to a total of $46,000,000,000. In other words, as the result of Roosevelt politics and policies, $25,000,-000,000 will be his legacy of debt to the business interests and to the people of this nation — for it is a debt the business interests and the people will have to pay.

Thinking you might be interested, here are some

of Mr. Roosevelt's annual statements regarding the fiscal affairs of the nation:

March 10, 1933: "There is reasonable prospect that within a year the income of government will be sufficient to cover the expenditures of government."
(As said, a moment ago, the debt was then approximately $21,000,000,000.)
January 4, 1934: "We should plan to have a definitely balanced budget for the third year of recovery, and from that time on to seek a continuing reduction of the national debt."

Government debt, March 1, 1933: $20,934,728,350. Government debt at close of first fiscal year under Mr. Roosevelt's management: $27,053,085,988. Increase: $6,118,-357,638.

January 7, 1935: "The Federal Government under present tax schedules will not need new taxes, or increased rates in existing taxes, to meet the expense of its necessary annual operations, and to retire its public debt."

Government debt, at close of first fiscal year: $27,053,085,-988. Government debt at close of second fiscal year under Mr. Roosevelt's management: $28,701,167,092. Increase: $1,648,081,104.

January 6, 1936: "Our policy is succeeding. The figures prove it. Secure in the knowledge that steadily decreasing deficits will turn in time to steadily increasing surpluses, and that it is the deficit of today which is making possible the surpluses of tomorrow, let us pursue the course we have mapped."

Government debt, end of second fiscal year: $28,701,167,-092. Government debt at close of third fiscal year under Mr. Roosevelt's management: $33,545,384,622. Increase: $4,844,217,530.

January 8, 1937: "Although we must continue to spend substantial sums to provide work for those whom industry has not yet absorbed, the 1938 budget is in balance; and, except for debt reductions of $401,515,-000, it will remain in balance even if later on there are included additional expenditures of as much as $1,537,-123,000 for recovery and relief."

Government debt, end of third fiscal year: $33,545,384,-622. Government debt at close of fourth fiscal year under Mr. Roosevelt's management: $36,427,091,021. Increase: $2,881,706,399.

January 5, 1938: "While I re-emphasize the difficulty of estimating the revenue of the Federal Government from six to eighteen months before that revenue flows in, there is satisfaction in knowing that during the past four years the estimates of tax receipts thus made far in advance, have been infinitely more accurate as proven by the final result of the preceding years."

Government debt, end of fourth fiscal year: $36,427,091,-021. Government debt at close of fifth fiscal year under Mr. Roosevelt's management: $37,604,000,000.* Probable increase: $176,908,979.

Thinking, also, you might be interested in participating in this game (after all, it is your money) here are some blank spaces which you can fill in at your convenience in anticipation of the annual statements of 1939 and 1940:

January –, 1939:

Government debt, at close of fifth fiscal year:
Government debt at close of sixth fiscal year of Mr. Roosevelt's management: Probable increase:

* Budget Estimate.

January –, 1940:

Government debt, at close of sixth fiscal year:
Government debt at close of seventh fiscal year of Mr.
Roosevelt's management:
Probable increase:

Mr. Roosevelt was on safe ground — and business and the American people were on safe ground with him — when, in Pittsburgh, in October 1932, he said:

"Our federal extravagance and improvidence bear a double evil; our whole people and our business cannot carry on its excessive burdens of taxation; second, our credit structure is impaired by the unorthodox federal financing made necessary by the unprecedented magnitude of these deficits."

And, again, on March 10, 1933, when he said:

"Upon the unimpaired credit of the United States Government rests the safety of deposits, the security of insurance policies, the activity of industrial enterprises, the value of our agricultural products and the availability of employment.

"The credit of the United States Government definitely affects these fundamental human values. It, therefore, becomes our first concern to make secure the foundation. National recovery depends upon it.

"Too often in recent history liberal governments have been wrecked on rocks of loose fiscal policy. We must avoid this danger."

The second quotation is taken from his message to Congress when he was pleading for "powers to enable him to handle the entire problem of public expenditures." In that message can be found a paragraph which you might like to read once more:

"If the Congress chooses to vest me with this responsibility it will be exercised in a spirit of justice to all, of sympathy to those who are in need and of maintaining inviolate the basic welfare of the United States."

Looking back over pre-election promises and post-election performances, one wonders what Mr. Roosevelt meant when in Butte, Montana, in September 1932, he measured "the way we do things, not just the way we say things," as a "test of a man's sincerity."

Still, he may not have intended that people should pay too much attention to a mere promise in a mere political speech. He may have intended they look into the record of what he did, rather than the record of what he said. If so, here, briefly, is his spending record as Governor of the State of New York through the years from 1929 to 1932, inclusive:

Assuming office he found a surplus of $90,000,000 in the state Treasury.

At the expiration of his two terms there was a deficit of $96,000,000.

When he first took office the net debt of the state was $255,000,000.

At the expiration of his two terms the net debt of the state was $422,000,000.

That doesn't fit in with his concern over "liberal governments being wrecked on the rocks of loose fiscal policy." That doesn't square with his spoken anguish about "taxes being paid in the sweat of every man who labors." The kindest thing that can be said about Mr. Roosevelt's utterances is that he deals in words of double meaning.

But there are no words of double meaning in this statement: If through his tax program, Mr. Roosevelt is successful in his assault against business this nation will cease to be a democracy.

Nor, can it be said with any comforting degree of assurance that he will not be successful.

He is determined to have his own way. As determined as the little rich boy who not only wants to manage and pitch, but also wants to be the umpire, because he is the little rich boy who owns the baseball and who has distributed lollypops among the spectators. A lot of the spectators seem not to realize they could buy more lollypops if, instead of paying admission to see Mr. Roosevelt do all three things — manage, pitch and umpire — they kept their money and spent it themselves.

Forty billions of dollars is a lot of money to spend in less than five years. Sixty-five billions of dollars is a whole lot more.

In spending all this money belonging to all the people, the political opportunity to entrench deeper and still deeper into a position of permanency has not been overlooked.

This is the reason for saying it cannot be stated with any comforting degree of assurance that Mr. Roosevelt will not be successful.

As the people who supply this money, it is essential that we look up the answer to the question of how we supply it.

Sixty-five billions of dollars is a sum of money the imagination cannot grasp. Also, forty billions of dollars is a sum of money the imagination cannot grasp, although the mind tells us that forty billions of dollars is very much less than seventy billions of dollars. One billion dollars is a third sum of money the imagination cannot grasp, although the mind knows, too, it is a far lesser sum than forty billions of dollars. Even one million dollars is far beyond the imaginations of most of us, although, too, we all know that sum is much less than one billion dollars. As a matter of fact, to the great majority of us as individuals one thousand dollars is about the most any one of us is able to save, free and clear, out of a lifetime of work.

It is in our own interest, if not in the interest of business, that we see how this money has been, is, and will be collected.

It is collected from us in the form of taxes. It is collected from the rich and high-salaried individuals among us in the form of property, inheritance and income taxes. It is collected from all the rest of us in the form of hidden taxes. It was these taxes — these hidden taxes — Mr. Roosevelt was referring to, specifically, when he said "taxes are paid in sweat."

Under Mr. Roosevelt hidden taxes have risen to the point where they now account for at least $33\frac{1}{3}$

per cent of all taxes. The likelihood is that this figure of 33⅓ is low. The chances are the actual figure is closer to 40 per cent. For the most part, these are taxes that are levied on the people who can least afford to pay. These are people who are the wage earners — men and women in jobs which pay from $25 to $30 a week.

You and I — every one of us — contribute our dollars, our dimes, our nickels and our pennies that these billions may be collected for him to spend. Our dollars in income and pay-roll taxes and our dimes and nickels and pennies that are paid in taxes on everything else.

Today — and for a long time into the future — every time anybody spends so much as one dollar, or so little as one cent, he, or she, contributes some part of that same money to the tax collector.

It doesn't make the slightest difference what the money is spent for, taxes are hidden in everything that is bought. Nor, can the tax collector be avoided by trying to save. If the penny is put into a child's toy bank, taxes were collected when the bank was purchased. If the dollar is kept in purse, or pants pocket, taxes were collected when the purse, or the pants, were bought. If the penny, or the dollar, is put into a savings bank, the taxes levied on the savings bank are deducted from the interest normally paid, and the saver is credited with the difference.

The hard, though distressing, fact is:

The wage earners are paying more in taxes, proportionate to their actual needs, than are those in the higher income brackets.

For illustrative purposes, let us say a person has an income of $50,000 a year. For easy figuring, his taxes can be put at $20,000 a year. This leaves him $30,000. Surely, on an income of $30,000 a year he is not going to be hungry, nor ill-clad, nor lack shelter. If he does, it is his choice.

On the other hand, a person earning $25 or $30 a week also pays hidden taxes. It is likely he will pay as much in them as does his more prosperous fellow citizen. After all, no matter what a person's income he can only eat so much, can only wear one suit of clothes at a time, can only be in one place at a time.

Without going into too much detail, it boils down to this:

To the family with an average income, hidden taxes very often mean the difference between having enough food on the table, enough milk, enough bread — and not having enough! They mean the difference between having, and not having, an extra ton of coal for the winter, a pair of shoes or a dress for the youngsters, a new coat or a new hat for the mother, a new suit for the father. Likewise, they may mean the difference between improper and proper attention when there is sickness in the family.

That is what paying these taxes that are hidden in everything every person buys means to the average family and theirs is no choice in the matter. The choice is with the politician. The truth of what Mr. Roosevelt said about "taxes and sweat" remains unchanged. The trouble is, Mr. Roosevelt has changed.

But the politician defends his tax collectors. He needs them to collect that he may spend. But he smudges this fact by crying out that life under our economic system has become so complex that Government has to take a hand to iron out the inequalities.

By pointing his finger at the economic system, and calling it complex, the politician is going through the routine of distracting attention from himself. What he should do is something he never does, and that is this:

Point his finger at our Government, and its tax-collecting system.

There is something that really is complex.

Nor is this the only way the New Deal clips "every man who labors." Not content with tricking him into paying billions of dollars each year in hidden taxes, it tunnels under him from another direction. By imposing continuously heavier taxes on his employer, it makes his own job far less secure; and, if he is out of a job, it greatly reduces his chances for getting one.

By being compelled to pay the tax collector before he meets his payroll — and, make no mistake about it, the Government demands that it be paid first — it means there is that much less money (*a*) to pay those already at work; (*b*) to employ additional people; and (*c*) to pay higher wages.

What rapidly increasing taxes mean can be seen from the 1937 report of a typical American company. In part, the report says:

"The management is gravely concerned with the growing burden of taxation. Our consolidated tax bill in 1937 reached $3,441,609, which exceeded the tax bill for any preceding year by a wide margin. It compares with a tax bill of $2,514,629 in 1936 and $1,275,421 in 1935. In the two-year period, the Company's tax bill increased 169.8 per cent.

"Approached from another angle, our taxes for the year 1937 amounted to 10.2 per cent of the consolidated pay-roll, or about ten cents for every dollar that was paid in wages and salaries during the year. While income increased 27.8 per cent, taxes increased 36.9 per cent during the year."

This company is one that in the more than thirty years of its existence has never had a strike. It is the principal support of an entire midwestern community. Like practically all American companies, it draws its executives from the ranks of its employes. Like practically all American companies, it does not pay "starvation wages." Like practically all American companies, it does not impose "sweat shop" conditions on its people. The men who manage this business are no different from the men who manage practically all American business.

They are men who believe that once this country is permitted to move normally, their real problem

will be one of finding men for jobs, rather than finding jobs for men.   They are business men who want
to press future plans with confidence that crack-pot
legislation and tax schemes will not destroy —
crack-pot tax schemes such as the Undistributed
Profits Tax, and the Capital Gains Tax, which were
imposed upon business by the will of Mr. Roosevelt.
There are more taxes that affect the pay envelope
of the workingman.   1702247

Social Security.

Here is a political football that has been kicked
all over the lot, without once going between the
goal posts.   Like so much New Deal legislation it
was written in haste, without sufficient knowledge
of the facts; and, for that matter, without very
much attention being paid to the facts already available when the law was written.

The mere statement that under its provisions the
Federal Administration is permitted to use — and
does use! — the collected taxes for the daily running expenses of government should be enough to
condemn its present form without further detail.

As to its effect on business, it is causing unemployment all along the line.   Especially is this true in the
smaller companies.   To these companies this tax
has been a severe burden because they have not been
able to pass it along.   Ordinarily, their output con-
sists of articles on which prices have been fixed for
quite a long time.   Not being in a position to ab-
sorb the tax, they have been compelled to reduce the

size of their working organizations. I have no idea of the amount of unemployment directly attributable to the imposition of this tax, but it must be a great deal.

The simple fact is: This law will have to be rewritten, if it is ever going to work.

As now in effect, its terms call for steadily increasing taxes over the next eleven years. That may mean more, and still more, unemployment, year by year.

Capital Gains Tax.

Here is a tax that was unjust in its conception, but which has been corrected to a large extent, by recent legislation. It was Mr. Roosevelt who insisted that it be imposed in its destructive form; Congress, at his insistence, imposed it. It was a tax clearly designed to appeal to mob prejudice.

Under it, the successful were penalized out of all proportion to their success. For illustration, a certain man had a salary, in 1937, of $100,000. His was one of the names you saw listed in the newspapers. Perhaps, when you saw his name, and his salary of $100,000, you said to yourself: "Wouldn't I like to be in his boots? You'd never hear me kicking about paying taxes to the Government."

Well, let's see. In 1937 this man lost, on account of being forced to sell various securities, $125,000. Under the Capital Gains Tax, his deductible capital losses were limited to $2000. He was forced to pay an income tax on $98,000. He did not have the money to pay the tax. He was compelled to borrow it. His notes are still outstanding, although he is slowly paying them off. Actually, instead of having a taxable income of $98,000, in 1937, he had a net loss of $25,000.

Would you still like to be in his boots?

The manner in which the capital net losses and gains were handled under this revenue act caused people to hold on to securities when they should have sold them. It had a serious effect on the liquidity of the market, all of which affected employment and the business outlook.

Undistributed Profits Tax.

Without question, this was one of the worst pieces of tax legislation ever imposed upon the tax-paying people of this nation. Despite the statements of Mr. Roosevelt, it is a tax that is thoroughly wrong in principle. True, its penalties have been changed by Congress but, at Mr. Roosevelt's insistence, the principle has been retained.

It is a tax principle that practically forces a company to pay out all its earnings, saving nothing for the inevitable "rainy day." It was a tax that was particularly bad for small companies. Most small companies felt they were not in a position to pay tax up to 27 per cent, in order to retain earnings which were needed in their businesses. Therefore, they paid out all their earnings with the result that they now find themselves much in need of capital.

Because of the strict rules of the Securities Exchange Commission, it is practically impossible for a small company to do any financing. The cost is too great. Consequently, as a result of having paid out all their earnings in dividends, the great majority of them are now in distress. This distress has been communicated to their employes, with the inevitable result that payrolls have been cut drastically on the thin chance that the concerns will be able to remain in business.

But, Mr. Roosevelt, in spite of this distress, felt himself compelled to write to Senator Harrison and Congressman Doughton as follows:

"The Treasury stands to lose where the corporation does not distribute earnings, whereas if earnings were distributed the Treasury would collect additional taxes on the personal income tax returns of the stockholders."

Apparently, Mr. Roosevelt believes the Federal Government has title to a first lien on the citizen's earnings. Or, possibly, he believes it an act of mercy on the part of the Treasury when it allows the citizen to retain any part of his income.

From another point of view, what is there to say for a man who so loses his sense of proportion that he dispatches a message from the White House to the people's representatives while these same representatives are in the midst of revising this tax measure? Under the Constitution, tax measures originate in Congress. Under the Constitution, changes in tax laws are made in Congress. Under the Con-

stitution, tax measures do not fall among the pre-
scribed duties of the Executive.

But frantic to spend, apparently Mr. Roosevelt
became fearful the tax burden might be lessened,
thus furnishing him with less money. All in all,
it was an illuminating insight into his mind.

Repeatedly, however, we hear from the White
House complaints over the "poverty of ideas" coming from business men regarding the present depression. Also, we hear the same sort of lamenting
from New Deal Senators and Congressmen. Just
recently one of these senators, in discussing hearings before a special committee, proclaimed, under
a Washington date line:

"The thing about the hearings which impresses me is
the poverty of ideas expressed by the many distinguished
leaders of business, finance and industry regarding the
recession, its effects and the remedies to be proposed for
its cure."

Even the *New York Times,* which has swallowed
a good many New Deal utterances, gagged on this
one, and was moved to comment, editorially:

"This raises the question of what constitutes an 'idea'
in the current parlance of Washington. The various
merchants and manufacturers and bankers who appeared
before the committee at its many sessions had much to
say of the causes of the recession. They had many pro-
posals to offer for its cure. They recommended, among
other things, that the Government put its fiscal affairs
in order, that it make peace with the utilities, that it

clarify its position in the matter of monopolies, that it revise tax laws which have plainly discouraged capital, that it set a definite limit to competition with private enterprise, that it revise a partisan labor law, and that it permit and encourage a better equilibrium throughout the structure of wages, costs and prices.

"But in the opinion of this disappointed Senator — and, it must be said, in the opinion of many of his colleagues and of a strong faction of the President's advisors — these various recommendations do not qualify as real 'ideas.' Why not? Because they propose no experiments in Government regulation, Government intervention, Government supervision, Government prestidigitation. Because they promise to create no new bureaus of busy Federal officials charged with the responsibility of informing business men how their businesses ought really to be run. Because they call for no new vast borrowing, no new vast spending, no new manipulation of the currency, up or down. Because they offer no single glittering new formula for ending the depression all at once, by the waving of a magic wand. Because, instead of being any one of these things, they are merely quiet, commonplace and oft-repeated recommendations for restoring business confidence by dealing directly with causes which have destroyed it."

But Mr. Roosevelt, in his radio utterances, tries to assure us that increasing prosperity will take care of his additional spending and also, take care of the tax burden he has already put upon the backs of the people; that, as the people, we will not notice the cost. This sort of talk is poppycock.

One hundred dollars is an appreciable sum of money to the average American family. It will continue to be an appreciable sum of money. The average American family doesn't know it but right today it is paying out considerably more than $100 each year in hidden taxes. Nor does it know that the more spending the Federal Government does, the greater will be these same hidden taxes.

As for the owners and managers of American business, the tax laws have them gripped in a vice from which there is no escape excepting through a realization by enough of the people that the New Deal tax laws are more destructive to their welfare and their democratic form of government than any raid the Executive has made upon the rights of Congress, more destructive than Mr. Roosevelt's attempt to pack the Supreme Court, more destructive than his effort to reorganize the agencies of the Government.

The plain truth is that the Constitution, the Courts, the Congress and the people will all go by the board when taxes reach the point where the people can no longer pay.

The one sure way to bring Fascism to this country is through prolonged government spending of large sums of borrowed money. No nation, not even this nation, can continue living far beyond its income without eventually exhausting its credit. When credit is exhausted collapse follows. Dictatorship arrives.

4

Another thing which is causing widespread unemployment is the Wagner Act, along with its subsidiary, the National Labor Relations Board, which was set up to interpret and enforce this legislation.

The Wagner Act is a law that was whipped through Congress at the insistence of John L. Lewis, head of the CIO. It was signed by Mr. Roosevelt; and, when signing, Mr. Roosevelt hailed it as "a national labor policy."

It is no such thing.

It is a law that violates, in almost every particular, the most fundamental principle in our democracy, that of fair play, and equality, before the law.

It is a law that has fomented more strikes, more labor disturbances, more dissension and more class feeling than any piece of legislation ever written into the statute books of the United States.

It is a thoroughly one-sided law which defines unfair and illegal actions by employers, and fixes the punishment for violation, but completely fails to define, or punish, any unfair, or illegal act by labor organizations.

Some day American labor — and especially that

part of labor presently aligned with him — will start looking into John L. Lewis's record, and will come to realize that he is nothing more than a labor politician — a labor politician who knows a great deal about how to create turmoil, but very little about how to build understanding.

John L. Lewis is the labor politician who, in his lust for power, did his considerable part in throwing this nation back into depression; for there can be no disputing the fact that the present depression first began creeping, and then began taking its first heavy steps across the nation from the automobile factories in Michigan, and the succession of strikes that stopped production lines. To John L. Lewis belongs the credit for those strikes; and no one should try to take it from him.

Just as no one should try to take any credit from Madam Perkins, Secretary of Labor, for her assistance, and for this little gem of whimsicality, which was given to posterity on January 26, 1937:

"The legality of the sit-down strike has yet to be determined."

As no one should try to take any credit, for his assistance, from Postmaster General James Farley who could see nothing to really be concerned over when strikers stopped delivery of United States mails through CIO picket lines around steel plants in Ohio.

As no one should try to take any credit, for his assistance, from Mr. Roosevelt who, after weeks of silence regarding the strikes, cried: "A plague on both their houses."

Before proceeding further, however, I should like to make some things perfectly clear:

I approach the problem of labor relations as a man who came from the ranks of labor. I know from personal experience what it means to support a family on a low wage. Ever since I became an employer of labor I have practised collective bargaining. I believe thoroughly in that principle. I am gratified that the principle of collective bargaining has been declared constitutional by the Supreme Court of the United States.

But I also believe there are other rights which must be considered, in addition to the principle of collective bargaining. The right to strike is confirmed in the law. But the right to work should likewise be confirmed. If protection is thrown around the right to strike — as it is! — the same protection should be thrown around the right to work.

Protection should be given the workingman from the exploiting types of employers — and, also, from the exploiting types of union organizers, and so-called labor leaders. And in addition to giving protection to the man who wants to strike, as well as the man who wants to work, we must give protection to the third party which always pays the big share of the cost in every labor dispute. That third party is the public. Under the Wagner Act there is no protection for the man who wants to work, and there is no protection for the public. How can it be called "a national labor policy?"

The aim of labor legislation should be to bring about co-operation between all three parties. Unless it does, it fails.

In contrast with the record of turmoil of the CIO, under John L. Lewis, there is this statement of the American Federation of Labor:

"The American Federation of Labor wants peace. It did everything possible short of submitting to minority rule to avert war. Despite repeated attempts at peaceful negotiation with the CIO, the A. F. of L. found itself balked by the imperious will of one man — John Lewis. While these futile negotiations were in progress, the American Federation of Labor, under the leadership of President Green, marshalled a large force of organizers and went to work in an orderly, disciplined way. It gained more than a million members, and still has them. It did not resort to sit-down strikes, or other illegal methods. It respected contracts. It entrenched itself in the confidence of the workers, the employers, and the public."

I am happy to reprint that statement here, in some acknowledgment of more than thirty years of fair dealing with the American Federation of Labor.

The American Federation of Labor recognizes the rights of employers, the sanctity of contracts, the property of others, the one-sidedness of the Wagner Act, and the lop-sidedness of the National Labor Relations Board. John L. Lewis recognizes none of these things. He only knows that the Wagner Act has given him a horse to ride. That horse is American business. Using the National Labor Relations Board as both whip and spur, he is riding hard.

Next to heavy taxation, the presence of strikes — or the constant threat of them — does more to cripple business, or destroy it completely, than any other cause.

Mr. Roosevelt would have you believe differently. His is the theory that Government spending creates prosperity; and the more spending the more prosperity. Mr. Roosevelt dismisses, with a wave of the hand and a smile, the fact that strikes, and the constant threat of them, have contributed, greatly, to the depression.

In his radio talk on the evening of April 14, 1938, he gave his conclusions about the causes for the depression, thus:

"There were many reasons; one of them was fear — fear of war abroad, fear of inflation, fear of nationwide strikes. None of these fears has been borne out."

Apparently Mr. Roosevelt did not consult the State Department, the Treasury Department, nor the Department of Labor in preparation for his speech.

The State Department could have told him about the War in Spain, and the War in China, and the fear of war in Central Europe, in case he missed reading about those things on the front page of the newspapers.

The Treasury Department could have told him about its contemplated action — announced but a few hours after Mr. Roosevelt was on the radio — of desterilizing $1,500,000,000 in gold; in fact, he, himself, in that same speech spoke of an action in April 1937 when, to quote his words, "the Federal Reserve System curtailed banking credit, and the Treasury commenced to sterilize gold as a further brake on what it was feared might turn into a runaway inflation." So, in April 1937, the Administration itself had the same fears business men had regarding inflation.

The Department of Labor could have told Mr. Roosevelt that in numbers of strikes, as well as in numbers of people directly affected, we had more labor disturbances in 1937 than in any previous year in our history. In number of strikes, there were 4470; in all, 1,860,621 people were directly involved. As a result of those strikes, 1,860,621 wage earners lost 28,000,000 workdays.

In fairness to Mr. Roosevelt it should be noted that later on in his talk he did speak of lost workdays. "Lost working time is lost money," he said. "Every day that a workingman is unemployed, or a machine is unused, or a business organization is marking time, it is a loss to the nation." He used those words in referring to the depression that set in in 1929.

Still another thing that upsets the business equilibrium of the nation is Mr. Roosevelt's capriciousness regarding legislation.

Several years ago the late Louis McHenry Howe, Mr. Roosevelt's secretary, is reported to have spoken of his employer this way:

"He has to have a new toy every day, and one of my jobs has been to keep toys away from him on which he could cut himself."

If Howe said this he did so with no unkind intent. The fact is, he couldn't have had an unkind thought regarding Mr. Roosevelt because he was too close to him, as an employe; and too fond of him, as a friend. But, realistic always, Howe recognized Mr. Roosevelt's mind as a restless mind. As a mind that always wanted change — change for the better, if possible, but, whatever the circumstances, change.

In those twenty-eight words — "he has to have a new toy every day, and one of my jobs has been to keep toys away from him on which he could cut himself" — Howe probably gave the best analysis of Mr. Roosevelt that has been given.

It explains, completely, Mr. Roosevelt's disregard of things he said yesterday as against what he says today; or says today as against what he may say tomorrow.

How else can his capriciousness in acts and words — acts and words such as these — be explained?

On January 3, 1936, in discussing the New Deal, he said:

"We had to build, you in the Congress and I, as the Executive, upon a broad base. Now, after thirty-four months of work, we contemplate a fairly rounded whole."

If those words meant anything, they meant the New Deal structure was about complete.

They implied a promise to business, large and small, that the days of harassment were pretty much ended, that the reforms Mr. Roosevelt "had in mind long before he was even nominated for the Presidency" had been effected.

It was an invitation for business men to come into their new home, and be comfortable; and it was an assurance that they could press ahead with future plans in confidence that future legislation would not destroy them.

For a time it seemed this promise would be kept. During the political campaign of 1936, Mr. Roosevelt repeatedly assured business that he was its friend. "I believe, as I have always believed and I will always believe in private enterprise as the backbone of economic well-being in America," he said, and added, "The opportunities for private enterprise will continue to expand. The people of America have no quarrel with business."

These were assuring words. As the campaign proceeded Mr. Roosevelt not only promised business but he promised the people that if they would take out another four-year lease on the new governmental structure he had built for them the rent probably would be less and certainly would be no higher.

On those terms, and on those promises, the people renewed the lease in the November elections.

Scarcely was the lease signed, however, when the landlord, in the person of Mr. Roosevelt, was standing on the doorstep and protesting against the private initiative of business "as a cure for the deep-seated national ills."

"Well-intentioned as they may be," he said early in 1937, "they fail for four evident reasons: First, they see the problem from the point of view of their own business; second, they see the problem from the point of view of their own locality or region; third, they cannot act unanimously because they have no machinery for agreeing among themselves; and, finally, they have no power to bind the inevitable minority of chiselers within their own ranks."

That was an extraordinary statement for even Mr. Roosevelt to make because, when he was Governor of New York, in 1930, he pointed out:

"Let us remember that from the very beginning differences in climate, soil conditions, habits, and mode of living in states separated by thousands of miles . . . introduced many factors in each locality which have no existence in others; it is obvious that almost every new or old problem of government must be solved, if it is to be solved to the satisfaction of the people of the whole country, by each state in its own way."

If it is true — and, it is! — that "differences in climate, soil conditions, habits and mode of living in states separated by thousands of miles" affect problems of government, it is equally true of business.

For illustration, the problems confronting a merchant in San Diego, California, are very different from the problems confronting a merchant in Bangor, Maine. The difference in climate affects, greatly, the merchandise on the shelves of the two stores; neighborhood desires, wants and needs are different. There is the difference in rent, in labor costs, in standards of living in these two widely separated communities. The growing seasons are not the same. State laws are not the same. Prices are not the same — and these are but a few of the differences that exist and will continue to exist however much Mr. Roosevelt may protest.

It is true that business which is purely local has its very important effect on all the business a nation transacts. Probably 50,000,000 people are directly dependent for their livelihoods on strictly local business. Local businesses such as stores, garages, cleaning establishments, dairies, barber shops, real estate offices, office buildings — hundreds of thousands of small businesses in thousands of communities, all depending for their individual prosperity, and the prosperity of their individual communities, upon the business judgment of the men who own, or operate, them.

To say that these hundreds of thousands of small businesses located in thousands of communities can be operated better by master minds located in Washington does not border upon the ridiculous. It *is* ridiculous.

But Mr. Roosevelt doesn't seem to think so. It is unfortunate for him, and it is unfortunate for us, that Mr. Roosevelt has spent so much of his time in the hustings and so little of his time in the market place.

Were it otherwise, he would know that the great bulk of American business is small business, just as the great bulk of our cities are smaller cities, although New York and Chicago are better press-agented. He would know that practically ninety-eight per cent of American industries are small businesses — employing less than 500 men each. He would know that of the 200,000 factories in this country, 145,000 of them produce less than $100,-000 worth of goods a year each, and that each of these is owned by one individual, or a few individuals. He would know that of the 1,500,000 retail stores, 1,350,000 are small stores, and stores that are the property of one individual, or a few individuals.

These are but a few of the things in our national picture of business; and, in addition to knowing these things, Mr. Roosevelt would know if big business were eliminated that practically all small business would go with it; and, if small business were eliminated, big business could not exist.

The inescapable fact is, each depends upon the other.

The additional fact is, you cannot draw a dividing line through it, saying this part is undesirable and it must be eliminated. Once government begins doing this it winds up by eliminating all. Undesirable practices should, and must, be eradicated but, as someone has said, "it isn't necessary to burn the house to roast the pig."

The little business man knows those things. He also recognizes the Administration's solicitude for him as something false rather than as something real. For illustration, when the Undistributed Profits Tax was made into law, Mr. Roosevelt beckoned to the little business man, and holding forth his gift told him this was his charter of freedom.   Accepting the gift, which was all wrapped up in fancy red tape, the little business man found, too late, that it was a pair of handcuffs.

By experience he learned that the Undistributed Profits Tax was legislation designed to keep his business small, permanently; because, under it, his profits were seized by Government, thus preventing their use in expanding the business, and giving employment to more people.

That philosophy, written into law at the turn of the century, would have tended to freeze American industry at its 1900 level.

But Mr. Roosevelt is hipped over "planned economy," just as he is hipped with the idea that the processes which make a big business man out of a little business man likewise change that same man into being a despot.   This "reasoning" could be followed with more fruitful results if applied to politics.

As an advocate of "planned economy," neither Mr. Roosevelt, his helpers nor any other proponent of this theory, has ever faced honestly — or told the people — that there is no such thing as a planned production to meet a free demand.

If production is controlled, then consumption must be rationed.

This means that everyone must spend his pennies, his dimes and his dollars at the command of a government bureaucrat.   In turn, it means the people have got to be told what to buy, how much to buy, and when to buy.   They must obey.   Otherwise, the whole scheme gets out of joint.

Beyond all that, "planned economy," stifles progress.   To make good the planners must anticipate, far in advance, people's tastes, and people's wants. For illustration, do you suppose any human being could have foretold, in 1900, what the automobile industry would become?   To successfully handle the future, with no present knowledge of what the future holds, is a problem, I am sure, that is beyond the reach of even the most ambitious among the New Dealers.

As said, none of them has had, nor will have, the courage to tell the people that if production on the farms, and in the factories, is to be controlled then all the people must cooperate and go to the public office-holder for ration cards.

But the Administration complains that greedy business men, in their hurry to make profits, allowed the wheels of production to over-run the wheels of consumption, thus causing the present depression. The Administration would take off these wheels — wheels that are known as Invention, Thrift, Work, and Independence, all being controlled by the steering wheel of Individual Initiative — and substitute for them the wheels of the New Deal — wheels which, in turn, are known by these names: Collectivism, Spending, Waste and Propaganda, with the steering wheel in the hands of a reckless driver called Bureaucracy.

The thing to do is to take the brakes off consumption. By another name these brakes can be identified as legislation. It is legislation enacted in the name of taxation. It is taxation that has imposed a heavy penalty on business. It is taxation that has greatly affected the general welfare of the American people. Two years ago, or even one year ago, many of our people were becoming deeply concerned about the New Deal's punishing tax legislation, and were worrying what would happen when depression came again.

Mr. Roosevelt wasn't worrying. As late as January 1936, he was saying, "there is today no doubt of the fundamental soundness of the policy of 1933. If we proceed along the path we have followed . . . we shall continue our successful progress during the coming years."

His mistakes still charm him. He still has no remedy excepting the tax remedy. But he still calls upon business to pick up the slack and put people back to work.

Until it is released from the straight-jacket Mr. Roosevelt has strapped about it business will not be able to do its natural part in restoring prosperity. Mr. Roosevelt knows this, but to confess it would be to confess he could be wrong.

But the situation is bigger than he is. It is bigger than politics. It is larger than business. It is bigger than all these because it is a situation that affects all the people.

5

The responsibility for this depression is clear. It rests with a political administration that for more than five years has taken the easy path of expediency out of all its difficulties.

To look back quickly on some policies, and then to focus on the recent months:

Banking. Mr. Roosevelt has not strengthened the banking system. On the contrary, he has weakened it. He has used it as a warehouse for Government bonds. In more ways than one, that is a cheerless thought. Even Marriner Eccles, the New Deal's Chairman of the Federal Reserve Board of Governors, admits "a major task of banking reform remains to be done." *

Currency. The Administration came into power pledged to "a sound currency to be preserved at all hazards." The tinkering with the currency began early. In July 1933, Mr. Roosevelt torpedoed the London Economic Conference by sending a message proposing "national currencies with the objective of . . . continuing purchasing power . . . in terms of the commodities and needs of modern civilization."

* April 1937, *Fortune Magazine.*

On January 31, 1934, the "sound currency that was to be preserved at all hazards," became a dollar devalued to 59.06 per cent of its former gold value. Today, and in his sole discretion, Mr. Roosevelt can cause to be issued $3,000,000,000 in greenbacks. In his sole discretion, he can put the United States on a bimetallic standard. In his sole discretion he can fix the value of the silver dollar at any ratio he sees fit.

The American dollar is anything but a sound dollar.

Agriculture. First, Mr. Roosevelt talked about a belt of trees and then when it was pointed out to him that trees never had grown where he wanted to put them, he decided that the solution to the farmer's troubles was not to be found in growing things — but, rather, was to be found in *not* growing things. As a result of getting cash awards for not growing things, the farmer is losing (1) his export market; and (2) his American market. The result is, everybody loses.

The farm problem is not a single problem. It is a multitude of problems. The answer will not be found in Secretary Wallace's objective of "a national granary."

Emerson foresaw that years ago when he wrote: "The harvest will be better preserved and go farther laid up in private bins, in each farmer's corn barns and each woman's basket, than if it were kept in national granaries."

So long as we suffer from the philosophy that nothing is national unless the government owns it, we will be continually on the retreat from prosperity.

Tariffs. Here is one place where the Administration has been doing, generally speaking, a constructive job. The rigidities that had been set up across the years had to be broken down. A most capable man was selected for the job. I do not agree with the authority that has been given Mr. Roosevelt to bargain. I do not agree with all the things that have been done. But, under difficulties that would have discouraged a lesser man, Secretary of State Hull stands out as one of the great statesmen of our times.

Labor. The labor policies of the New Deal are the policies of John L. Lewis, head of the CIO. Mr. Roosevelt needed Mr. Lewis, and his organization, for political purposes. Mr. Lewis delivered. Mr. Roosevelt delivered.

Taxation. This story traces back to the summer of 1933, when the spending began.

Now, for just a moment, I want to interrupt this recital of events, to make one thing perfectly clear:

To be concerned over the welfare of the American people, and their business interests, is a subject too high to be pulled down to a partisan level. Seeing this nation of ours as something to build is not to be political; and to view its hard-won resources as something to conserve is not to be partisan.

To make this nation prosperous, you can't fumigate thrift. You can't quarantine work. And you can't knock private initiative on the head. You can't continue to spend something you do not have. You can't squander your way to security. You can't take your debts, and call them assets.

I know, too, that bad laws will not work. A legislature can pass them, and a Supreme Court can uphold them, but unless they are good laws sooner, or later, the people will reject them. We have had more than our share of bad laws these recent years.

We came into the second Roosevelt Administration with a hangover of bad laws from the first Administration. With the elections over, Mr. Roosevelt should have sat down quietly, and taken stock. There was no occasion for hurry now, and he should have recommended that plainly unworkable legislation be rewritten in the light of experience. The huge majority he had received in the elections should have sobered him, should have made him want to take the people more into his confidence. Instead, he accepted his victory as a "mandate from the people;" and interpreted the "mandate" as blanket authority to do as he wished.

It was only a matter of weeks before he was sending a bill to Congress demanding that the Supreme Court be enlarged to fifteen members. His propaganda agencies swung into heavy action. He joined the clamor himself by going on the radio to say "it was the American people themselves who want this furrow tilled."

Mr. Roosevelt completely misjudged the people. He did not realize, apparently, that he could get away with attacking the Court in speeches (although it is significant he made no attacks during the election campaign; in fact, he carefully avoided giving any expression as to his real views on the Court although repeatedly requested to do so) but when it came to attacking the Supreme Bench with direct action, that was something else again.

Immediately Senators and Congressmen were being bombarded with protests. In unmistakable terms the American people told Washington they wanted none of Mr. Roosevelt's "tilling in that furrow." After a hard fight in the Senate, the raid to capture the judiciary was beaten off.

The likelihood is, however, Mr. Roosevelt will return to the attack. In fact, at this writing, his Secretary of Agriculture is preparing the way by issuing statements and sending letters. He is doing so with Mr. Roosevelt's knowledge and with Mr. Roosevelt's consent.

It is a disturbing quality, but Mr. Roosevelt seems to delight in catching people off guard. One technique is to beat the drums of emergency and try to force legislation "now;" the other technique is to slip something across quietly. The inevitable result is that he has engendered a feeling that he has to be watched — and watched, continuously.

This is not a feeling the Chief Executive of a nation should arouse in a people.

It is a quality which has contributed to and which prolongs the depression.

Another quality is his own indecisiveness. It will sound strange to apply the term "indecisive" to

Mr. Roosevelt.   Nevertheless, it is the proper term.

Some men deliberate too long in wondering if the action indicated is the proper action — for economic reasons.   Mr. Roosevelt deliberates too long in wondering if the action indicated is the proper action — for political reasons.

As Governor of New York he displayed his indecisiveness by delaying his action in ousting James J. Walker as Mayor of the City of New York.   It was not until it was clear the decision would be beneficial to him politically that he acted.

As Chief Executive he displayed the same deliberateness in the Undistributed Profits Tax measure. His own advisors warned him that the measure was harmful to small business.   He seemed to be persuaded, but when Huey Long began menacing the political horizon Mr. Roosevelt rushed the Bill to Congress as *his* "share-the-wealth" plan.

Probably never before have we had in the White House a man so easily frightened by the scarecrows of politics.   He has wooed, assiduously, the Communists, and the Socialists, the "share-the-wealthers," the Silverites, the Greenbackers, the CIO'ers and every other type of pressure group.   In return for letting them into the Treasury, they have rewarded him with their votes.   When he could no longer woo them he has stolen their oratorical thunder and made it his legislative lightning.   Even now, in his second term, when ordinarily one would think his political fears would begin to disappear, and his political ambitions begin to lessen, we see him wooing the symbol of the LaFollettes.

This is another of his qualities that stands in the way of recovery. No one knows what theory he is going to embrace next, tagging it with a "must" for Congress to make into law.

In the spring of 1937, it was fear of runaway inflation that caused the Federal Reserve Board, acting under instructions from Mr. Roosevelt, to raise the reserve requirement of banks to the limit designated by law, and to continue to sterilize gold until the total reached approximately $1,500,000,000. This was a major deflationary step given almost without warning. By so doing Mr. Roosevelt injected a heavy dose of morphine into the veins of the financial system. It promptly went to sleep.

The depression began to be visible to the economists. It did not appear so the public could begin to see it until the late summer. It gained momentum rapidly but Mr. Roosevelt, instead of recognizing it for what it was, contented himself with a remark: "It all depends upon what newspaper one reads."

An "emergency session" of Congress was called. Mr. Roosevelt had in mind some laws he wanted passed. Congress, evidently acting under instructions, discussed the depression not at all. However, two handy prophets of the Administration did discuss it. Ickes and Jackson were ordered to the radio to abuse business for allowing the "recession" to happen.

Congress convened again early in January. Some among the people's representatives were determined to give the people the relief they so desperately needed. Over the objections of Mr. Roosevelt, two tax laws business men had been complaining so bitterly about were revised. Mr. Roosevelt, in retaliation, laid down a barrage of measures, such as the Reorganization Bill and the Wages and Hours Bill; and followed these retaliatory measures by calling upon Congress to turn over to him, for spending purposes, additional appropriations of more than $5,000,000,000.

The whole situation can be summed up this way:

As these words are written Congress has been in session more than seven months. The "emergency session" lasted two months; the present session has lasted more than five months. Never, in all this time, has there been an attempt on the part of Mr. Roosevelt to sit down, and seriously study with the Congress the causes for the existing hard times. After more than five years in office, he still has no remedy for economic ills excepting to spend.

Another quality which stands in the way of recovery is Mr. Roosevelt's determination to keep Government in business, in competition with its own citizens.

Everybody concerned knows that the stagnation in the capital and heavy goods markets is the result, in very large measure, of the New Deal's power policies. Not only does the New Deal spend hundreds of millions of dollars in constructing competing plants, but it lends municipalities other hundreds of millions of dollars so they may build their own systems to compete with private companies.

It is perfectly obvious that private investors will not lend their money to private utilities while such destruction continues. The utilities have repeatedly offered to spend several billions of dollars each year in expansion programs, thus furnishing steady employment to hundreds of thousands of men and women, if the Administration would issue a stop-order on its lending and spending in this field.

Mr. Roosevelt says "no." The destruction continues. The depression widens and deepens as a direct result.

It is unfortunate that Mr. Roosevelt's assault against the private ownership of property has not been dramatized for the American people as the Supreme Court issue and the Reorganization Bill were dramatized.

It is an issue of great importance.

Without our fully recognizing it, Mr. Roosevelt has taken us far along the path of Socialism. That path leads straight into Communism, Nazism, Fascism or whatever "ism" the fancy of the moment dictates it be called.

Certain it is if the American people are to continue along their own path, they will have to do it through their Congress — and through a Congress that is responsive to the economic needs of the nation.

And, aside from Mr. Roosevelt's political ambitions, is there any reason why we should not continue along our own path?

Here we are as a nation occupying but six per cent of the area of the globe and with but seven per cent of the world's population. Yet, we have 60 per cent of the telephones and telegraph facilities; 80 per cent of the automobiles; 70 per cent of the oil supplies; 60 per cent of the wheat and cotton; 50 per cent of the copper and pig iron; and nearly 67 per cent of the banking resources of the world. Along with those things — and they are but a few of our advantages — we have about 50 per cent of the world's gold supply, while our people have a purchasing power greater than the 500,000,000 inhabitants of Europe.

Yet, here we are, back in depression again, the direct result of political blundering by a group so bereft of political statesmanship that its only suggested remedy is:

Spend some more!

Let's glance at those percentages again, to see if we can translate some of them into individual possessions.

Take the ownership of an automobile, for illustration. If you are a wage earner, do you have one? If you do, then remember the chances are the wage earner in a similar job in any other country in the world hasn't one.

This applies all the way down the line, including radios, refrigerators, homes, electricity, bank accounts, insurance policies and foods that while common on your table are luxuries seldom seen on the tables of foreign wage earners.

Do all these things, and many more, exist in such abundance in socialistic countries such as Russia, Germany and Italy, where the people have surrendered their freedom as individuals in the hope that dictators will bring them greater economic security?

Of course not.

Not only have the peoples of these nations lost security, but they are being marched to war to fatten the ambitions of their leaders.

Is this what you want?

If it isn't then you do not want what you are headed for under the New Deal.   Socialism, to operate at all, requires government planning.   Government planning means dictatorship.

There was a time when Mr. Roosevelt believed differently than he now believes.   That was when he was merely a Governor of New York.   Then he said:

"The doctrine of regulation and legislation by 'master minds' in whose judgment and will all people may gladly and quietly acquiesce, has been too glaringly apparent at Washington during these last ten years.   Were it possible to find 'master minds' so unselfish, so willing to decide unhesitatingly against their own personal interests or private prejudices, men almost godlike in their ability to hold the scales of justice with an even hand, such a government might be to the interests of the country; but there are none such on our political horizon, and we cannot expect a complete reversal of all the teachings of history."

Mr. Roosevelt's own words, uttered in 1930, state the case against his own present deeds.

6

Business, and the people, went into the last depression with a surplus. Business, and the people, went into the present depression with little preparation. But out of this present depression a number of lost truths are being found again; and one of those truths is this truth:

There are but two roads down which a dollar can travel. It can travel the road to productive enterprise; or, it can travel the road to government bureaucracy.

The choice of which road the American people want their dollars to travel is going to be made — and, it is going to be made soon.

The way has been cleared to force this choice. Every Administrative source — from the highest to the lowest — has swung into action. Business is being blamed for the present depression, just as it was blamed for the previous depression. If, this time, the New Dealers succeed in making the blame stick, *there will be a different form of government in this country.*

No people, not even the American people, are going to continue to live in the midst of hard times. If the New Dealers convince the people that they can take over business, run it better, and free the people from anxiety this is the straw at which the people will grasp.

The people of other nations have grasped at the same straw — and, in grasping, have seen their democratic institutions of government disappear. Already, propaganda is beginning to appear in this country telling us that in nations where there are dictators there are no problems of unemployment and no idle factories. What does not show up in this propaganda is that at their best, the standards of living in these nations is below our standard at its worst.

Nor am I alone in my concern over the ambitions of Mr. Roosevelt. Frank R. Kent, one of the ablest students of politics in this country, pointed out in a recent issue of *The American Mercury:* "For the future, let the American voter keep his eye most carefully on the White House gentleman who has such an itch for totalitarian power."

As far back as June 26, 1937 we find Walter Lippmann, another able student of politics, writing in the *New York Herald Tribune:* "I wish I could recover the belief that the President is interested in democratic reforms and not in the establishment of irresistible power personally directed. It is not pleasant to have such fears about the Chief Magistrate of the Republic. But for many long months nothing has happened which helps to dispel these fears. Many, many things continue to happen which accentuate them."

General Hugh S. Johnson is still another able student. In discussing the reorganization bill in his newspaper column, General Johnson went to great pains to point out the bill was revolutionary, and the road to one-man government.

These three men — Kent, Lippmann, and Johnson — were all ardent supporters of Mr. Roosevelt in the early days of his administration.

As for Mr. Roosevelt, himself, he seems to shudder at the thought that anyone would, or could, suspect him of nursing dictatorial ambitions. Shudders so much that he routed newspapermen from their beds in Warm Springs, Georgia, at one o'clock in the morning of March 1, 1938, to proclaim: "I don't want to be a dictator."

Seeing his father under pressure, that smart young man, James Roosevelt, immediately used the White House as a sounding board to issue this statement:

"No dictator in the world today had any important part in the constitutional, parliamentary or democratic government which he superseded."

Hitler was Chancellor of the German Republic before he seized dictatorial powers.

Stalin was Chairman of the Politbureau before he seized dictatorial powers in Russia.

Vargas was President of Brazil before he seized dictatorial powers.

Carol was the constitutional king of Rumania before he seized dictatorial powers.

All in all, a lot of publicity has gone through the

typewriters of the New Deal seeking to assure the American people that Mr. Roosevelt has "none of the qualifications of a dictator."

But, to get back to that strange spectacle of one o'clock in the morning of March 1, in Warm Springs, Georgia.

What would cause Mr. Roosevelt to issue such a statement? Often he has said to those around him that he is the Administration's own best lightning-rod as to what the people are thinking. If that is true, then he must have sensed that the people were fearful. In turn, what would cause such fears? The answer to that question is, of course, Mr. Roosevelt, himself.

Let's go back to the beginnings of his administration to see if the people's fears are self-induced; or whether, as Mr. Roosevelt said in his early-morning protestation, the charge was made out of whole cloth.

1. On March 10, 1933, he captured control of the public purse when Congress vested in him "powers to handle the entire problem of public expenditures."
2. He can devalue the American dollar any time he pleases.
3. He can change our monetary standards at any time, putting the United States on a bimetallic standard, by decreeing the free and unlimited coinage of silver.
4. The value of the silver dollar can be fixed as he wishes.
5. He can issue $3,000,000,000 in notes (a) to reduce the Federal Government's debt; or (b) to purchase Government securities.
6. He can use the "stabilization fund" of the United

States Treasury in any way he sees fit, and his actions are "final, and not subject to review by any other officer of the United States."

7. He controls the rules and regulations affecting the conditions under which gold can be acquired and held, melted or treated, transported, imported or exported.

8. At any time he sees fit, he can suspend trading on every stock exchange for a period of 90 days.

9. In tariff matters he can raise, or lower, by 50 per cent the duties on any goods imported into the United States from any foreign country.

10. He can spend the billions appropriated for relief as he sees fit.

11. His is the final word on "prevailing rates of pay" for all those employed on federal works projects.

12. He determines the policies of relief agencies, no matter in what community they operate.

Those are but some of the powers in Mr. Roosevelt's personal keeping. Powers which are his alone to use and for the use of which he need account to no one. They are powers far greater than ever have been held by any American President. Little wonder the people are fearful when they know that the value of the dollar bill they have worked for, or saved, is subject to the will of one man.

But that is not all. Not nearly all. Here are some other acts of Mr. Roosevelt in his rush for more power:

(*a*) Through his National Industrial Recovery Act he tried to capture control of business.

(*b*) Through his Agricultural Adjustment Act he tried to capture control of the nation's food resources.

(c) Through his Supreme Court measure he tried to capture control of the judiciary.

(d) Through his Reorganization Bill he tried to capture control of the independent agencies of the Federal Government.

(e) Through the Wagner Act — and its interpretative body, the National Labor Relations Board — he is trying to capture control of labor.

(f) Through his letter to the tax-bill conference of the Senate-House Committee he displayed his wish to capture control of the taxing powers.

(g) Through his creating of a state of permanent "emergency" which gives him a chance to spend billions of dollars, he is afforded an opportunity to show the people's representatives how to influence votes and win elections.

(h) Through his use of public funds to maintain a propaganda bureau he is given an opportunity to extol the virtues of the New Deal; and to use the tar brush on all those who see its faults.

(i) Through the use of berating vocabularies he is dividing the American people into classes, by the technique of "always saving them from their enemies."

Stalin, Hitler and Mussolini are always saving the people from "their enemies." Stalin is always saving the Communists from the middle classes — and shooting unfaithful Communists. Hitler and Mussolini are always saving the Nazis and Fascists from the Communists — and sending unfaithful Nazis and Fascists to concentration camps.

Periodically, Mr. Roosevelt saves the American people from the "economic royalists" and the "feudalists" and sends unfaithful New Dealers to the political execution block.

Then there is this illuminating paragraph as written by Arthur Krock, one of Mr. Roosevelt's confidents, in the *New York Times*, on April 10, 1938:

"From March, 1933 until last January, Mr. Roosevelt decided what *he* wanted to do legislatively, had a bill prepared to carry out the ideas, and sent it ready-made to Congress to sign on the dotted line. . . Often his leaders introduced the measure without reading it. . . Always the rank and file of Congress knew nothing of the bill's contents until they read them in the newspapers. Sometimes, they did not trouble to do that, voting 'aye' on faith."

The Constitution of the United States provides that "the President shall from time to time give to the Congress information of the state of the Union and recommend to their consideration such measures as he shall judge necessary and expedient."

Under our Constitutional form of government, with its checks and balances, legislation is supposed to be written by the Congress instead of coming to it as a "must" order from the Executive.

Finally, there is the statement of Mr. Roosevelt himself. In January 1936, he sent to Congress a message containing this arresting declaration:

"In thirty-four months we have built up new instruments of public power. In the hands of a people's government this power is wholesome and proper. But in the hands of political puppets of an economic autocracy such power would provide shackles for the liberties of the people. . ."

But he seeks to quiet the people's fears by saying, "I have . . . too much knowledge of existing dictatorships to make me desire any form of dictatorship for a democracy like the United States."

Looking back over that by no means complete list of dictatorial powers now in his possession, a goodly share of the governmental affairs of the people are already in the hands of Mr. Roosevelt — instead of being, as Mr. Roosevelt says, "in the hands of a people's government."

The weight of his deeds adds nothing to the weight of his words; and what he has done subtracts greatly from what he says.

Mr. Roosevelt is a strange figure in the American scene. He has squandered the savings and the future earnings of not merely a part of our people — but all our people. He has broken practically every pledge he has ever made to the people. He has driven the people into another depression at a cost of 10,000,000 jobs, and at a loss of some $30,000,-000,000 in the market value of securities owned by approximately 12,500,000 stockholders. He has weakened the banking structure of the nation where some 48,000,000 of our people have deposited their savings. He has weakened the insurance companies with their 66,000,000 policy-holders. He is using the Social Security funds for the daily running expenses of his administration and as security for the appropriated savings is dropping IOU's into special funds in the United States Treasury. He has openly taunted the people about their Constitutional rights, and he has ridiculed the Supreme Court of the United States by adding to its membership a common scold, and a Ku Kluxer to boot.

And, still, he retains the affection, and the confidence, of large numbers of the American people.

Why is it?

Is it, as some say, because the American people no longer care about their freedom?

I am sure this is not true. The American people are already becoming aroused over the threat of dictatorship within their midst; and, as you have seen, Mr. Roosevelt knows they are becoming aroused.

Is it, as others say, because the American people have lost their power to become indignant over both misfeasance and malfeasance in public office?

I am sure this is not true, either. Just let the American people see wrong-doing in a government bureau such as, let's say, the TVA, or the PWA, or any other government agency. Plundering — either of funds or authority — may be covered up for a while but, eventually, it will be uncovered. See how quickly the American people will take care of that. As a case in point, the National Labor Relations Board is running for cover now.

Is it, as some say, because Congress surrendered so much of its authority that the people lost faith in their elected representatives?

There is a great deal of truth in this point of view. Generally speaking, for more than five years, we have had a Congress that has been sitting on its liver instead of getting to its feet. People will always turn to the one who acts and turn away from the one who sits. The best thing the American people can do for themselves, and for Mr. Roosevelt, is to send representatives to Washington who will serve the people. If, in the November elections the people send to Washington only those Senators and Representatives who serve Mr. Roosevelt, then they can blame only themselves if Mr. Roosevelt accepts it as a "mandate" and becomes a dictator in reality.

Is it, as others say, that the American people are unintelligent and are glad to let Mr. Roosevelt do their thinking for them?

This, certainly, is not true. In the first place, to call the American people unintelligent is to apply the term to one's self. You and I, as individuals, comprise the people. Inform us, and we will do our own thinking. Fail to inform us, and we will still do our own thinking.

Is it, as some say, because he has a gigantic propaganda bureau functioning from Washington?

This is an extremely important contribution. By dwelling on his human qualities — and he has many of them — the propagandists have created and developed affection; by dwelling on the good things he has done — and, there have been good things — while ignoring the bad things, the propagandists have created confidence.

Is it, as others say, because of the relief spending and the made work on government projects?

I am sure it isn't. It is true this personally controlled spending lines up millions of votes for the

New Deal, on the old theory that people "do not bite the hand that feeds them." As for creating confidence and affection, it fails. Human nature simply is not constituted that way. Most people resent being treated as paupers; those who do not resent such treatment resent the gift because it is not more.

Personally, I think the real reason for the confidence, and the affection, great numbers of the American people have for Mr. Roosevelt is found in none of the things mentioned.

I think the real reason is that Mr. Roosevelt, when he came into office, appealed to the best that was in all of us. Articulate, he rallied to his cause other men and women who perceived an opportunity to serve.

Among those who came were men and women of vision, of character, and of experience — men and women with trained minds who wanted to do nothing so much as they wanted to help. The Glasses, the Douglases, the Johnsons, the Warburgs, the Hulls — to name but a few. With these came others, the social spiritualists such as the Tugwells, the Berles, the Hopkinses, the Wallaces, the Lilienthals and the Perkinses — to name but a few of them. Bringing up the rear were the "get-while-the-getting-is-good-boys" of labor and politics — the Lewises, the Hagues of Jersey City, the Prendergasts of Kansas City, the Guffeys of Pennsylvania, the Nashes and the Kellys of Chicago — to name but a few of them. Thus it was that the administrative and legislative ends of the early New Deal was a conglomerate mixture of experience and inexperience, practical idealism and social spiritualism, realists in maintenance of government credit and realists in the political possibilities of government spending.

It wasn't long before the first group, which consisted of men and women who genuinely wanted to help and who were anxious to give of their time and their experience, were being told in words, and in deeds, that their presence was neither needed, nor wanted. Most of them got out; some remained, and work today under great difficulties.

The social spiritualists and the "get-while-the-getting-is-good-boys" of labor and politics were already inside the Treasury. The gap in the ranks caused by the departure of the first group was filled by stalwarts of invective — men such as Black and Ickes; and when Black was elevated to the Supreme Court, Jackson, Minton, and Schwellenbach came to fill his vacant chair.

Well, for a time, the social spiritualists ran helter-skelter through the Treasury — and helter-skelter from the Treasury with great gobs of the people's money dripping from their fingers. For them it was the most fantastic of their dreams come true; and what they did, in many cases with the billions of dollars they spent, was just as fantastic. But, they had their fling. As time passed most of them had to give way before the stampede of the realists of politics.

Realists who saw as New Dealer Senator Ashurst,

who once said on the floor of the Senate, "You are wise in getting money from Uncle Sam's Treasury while the getting is good."

Realists who are typified by Guffey, of Pennsylvania, whose attitude toward the New Deal is best expressed by his own words: "The fellows who've done the work I believe in rewarding."

And the realists who carry out the orders of the typical Guffeys. As, for illustration, John Laboon, a district organizer for the New Deal in Pennsylvania, who, at a meeting of WPA foremen and supervisors in Pittsburgh, laid down this law:

"Any WPA worker who is not in sympathy with the WPA program and the Roosevelt Administration will be eliminated from the WPA payrolls in this district as quickly as I can act. I want you men to report all such cases to me without delay."

Put together all the spending of the social stargazers and the spending of New Deal politics; add all the laws that have been written to punish and what has been produced is what you see:

Bread lines. Heavy taxes. Idle farms. Empty factories. Some 10,000,000 men and women out of work.

Many do not see it yet but some day the American people will realize that the New Deal, starting out to appeal to the best in us, now uses us to support the worst that is in politics.

No man, and no small group of men, and I do not care whether they are Republicans or Democrats,

New Dealers, or business men, can be trusted with practically unlimited power over the purse strings of the people.

No man, and no small group of men, thinking in the interest of the people, would want it.

No man, and no small group of men, are wise enough to handle it.

The sooner we restore the written checks and balances of our constitutional form of government, the better it is going to be for the people. The better it is going to be for those among us whom we select for public office.

The strength of government is found in the strength of the people who comprise it. To have a strong government the people, themselves, must always be stronger than those they choose to govern. Otherwise, it is a government that is dangerous for the people — but far more dangerous to those who govern.

This nation was built by the people, and not by transient political administrations. It came to be a great nation because its people came to be a great people; because, as a people, we have never believed in the theory that we should grow political giants and, ourselves, remain dwarfs.

If, in disagreeing with them, the New Dealers complain that I am not constructive, then, to them, I say:

All criticism which protests the seizure of powers by one man, or the surrender of powers to one man, is constructive criticism. What I am concerned with is the maintenance of our traditional American form of democratic government. This is a form of government that must be kept not only if we are to remain a free people, but if we are to be a prosperous people. It is an historical fact that the democratic nations are always the most prosperous nations. It is an historical fact that recovery from depressions always comes quicker in democratic nations than it does in nations where gigantic political blunders monopolize the economic field.

In our own country we have all witnessed political blundering that has sterilized individual effort, individual thrift and individual initiative. Recovery begins, not in legislative halls, but in every man's workshop. And every man's workshop is within himself — his own desires, his own ambitions, his own thrift, his own initiative and his own job. All government can ever do to preserve economic life is to allow natural laws to govern. Sooner, or later, these natural laws *will* govern — and that government which serves best is one that recognizes its own limitations.

The greatest contribution Mr. Roosevelt can make to the welfare of the American people is to recognize that fact — and let it operate. Otherwise, historians of some fifty or a hundred years hence, are likely to be writing something like this:

"Franklin D. Roosevelt made one great contribution to the people of the United States. He made them deeply conscious of the existence of their own Federal Government, and deeply concerned with its preservation."